Published in Great Britain in 2020 by Matthew
Cash /Burdizzo Bards Walsall, UK
Burdizzo Bards is part of the Burdizzo Books
Family.

COME AND RAISE DEMONS

MATTHEW CASH

Foreword - Al Barz

Every dip into these pieces will be like 'apple-bobbing'. You know you're going to get your face wet. And sometimes pricked because, if you know Matty-Bob Cash, you'll be aware that these are not apples, but more the fruits of a chestnut tree in their spiky shells. You'll be familiar with the taste, and that inside the prickly balls and leathery skins lies a mix of nutrition and nuttiness.

Matty-Bob's normal genre in the world of horror fiction seeps through, particularly in the 'Totally Hardcore Blackbird' and, although 'found poetry' tends to limit the writer, it is wafted at in 'Birmingham to Coventry' with "Kerryman motherclucker", "Freeze your fat", and "Eat here, Day crèche fried chicken".

There are also reimagined nods to a handful of famous lyrics where good gives way to bad or lust to gluttony and the chestnutty nuggets are broadcast throughout whether roasted or creamed in such phrases as "the rain-spattered tag of a floral tribute" and "Happiness is an airborne infection".

Matty-Bob points his invective and sprays fiercely, or sometimes with huge parental and spousal love or with the echoes of a cackle resounding. First glance it may seem this collection's better in his voice at a local pub or bookshop gig, and there is some extra nuance to be had there. But then first glance you wouldn't go spiky-chestnut-bobbing, and you would be unmistakenly poorer for that.

The strength of expletives is often lost in places where they arrive in every utterance. But Mr. Cash saves them up, like racemes of chestnut flowers blooming when the season is ripe. If you're allergic, watch out for Spring! As to the self criticism, "My poetry is never serious", I beg to differ.

Al Barz

MY Foreword

I don't know how long I've actually been writing
poetry. When writing forewords for my fiction I can
always pretty much pinpoint my story writing to as
early as possible. As soon as I discover a love for
something a part of my wants to either recreate it
with my own spin or completely reinvent it.
I suppose I would have studied poetry of some form
at school however High School is my earliest
recollection of ever creating any of my own. To begin
with a lot of my early poems were mammoth pieces,
basically stories that rhymed, it took me a few years
to break away from that pattern, even though I still
find it's sometimes an easier medium to get an idea
out than writing an actual story.
It wasn't until I began hanging around alleyways
with the likes of Richard Archer, Al Barz and Paul
Elwell that I started taking poetry seriously. They
groomed me with their vowels and rich consonants,
with promises of good, thrilling encounters with
quickfire, hot, back street prose. I was hooked,
beguiled by the mystical world that was opened up
to me, a world I'd only taken a glimpse at in my
teenage years.

I became familiar with the urchins that loitered behind the now shuttered infamous independent bookshop of Walsall, Matt Humphries, who lived in a dustbin like Oscar the Grouch from Sesame Street, Ian Davies, a crazed eyed mystic akin to that fucking weirdo caterpillar in Alice in Wonderland, Richard Archer, like a cross between Homer Simpson and John McClane but with a Black Country twist.
 And looming over them, two wizened wizards of words; Masters Elwell and Barz, a duo of poetry gods gazing down upon us bottom dwellers who foraged amongst the detritus for any dropped verbs or pronouns.

Umm...yeah...it got a bit weird then didn't it? Sorry, that happens from time to time. I have a fondness for typing the first thing that comes out of my fingers, I love it. Improv bullshit. I could do it now. I could do a magic, improv, totally stupid nonsensical poem right here in the foreword. Why? Because it's *MY* book, that's why! *My rules, babwy*. Yeah, I've even spelt 'baby' with a fucking 'w,' that's just how badass I am. I'm gonna write eight lines of improv shite[1] right now and I'm not even going to edit it. It maybe dire. Ready?

The walls won't hear you when your screaming's done
I can't abide the way you drown me with your pain
I'm afraid of having you back
Join me now if you're a stranger
I'll wait for you to come over to me

---

[1] This book's first example of an 'autofill' poem, actually.

Evil is the best thing for all of us
Buy your own soul here and you can find happiness
You love but you can't afford it

Well, fucking hell that all got a bit deep and emo
didn't it?
On with the book!
Matty-Bob

Found Poetry

When I first started taking poetry seriously Paul Elwell, a world-famous poet from the West Midlands, taught me not to take it seriously. He also inadvertently taught me the basics of 'found poetry' and how to make poetry out of the words that surround us.

Words are everywhere, I bet if you looked up from whatever version of this you are reading, wherever you are, there will be words in view, somewhere. In my livingroom, I just glanced quickly and caught the words 'Bepanthen' - a great healing, antiseptic cream, from a free samples set my wife had sent through the post that's sat on the fireplace, and 'Tango,' from the pop bottle on our coffee table. Just adding these two words together conjures up images of freshly tattooed couples dancing a tango, their newly inked skin oily with the popular cream used for tattoo aftercare. Not that amazing, I know, but it's just an example of spontaneous found words and the power they can sometimes have over your, well, my imagination.

During the summer holidays we went on a lot of bus journeys. I have a son called Mortimer who is a bus enthusiast and to pass long journeys I would randomly snatch words I saw out of the window. I would try to eliminate place names, unless they were particularly interesting to me, and I would collect them and write them down in the order I saw them, making sure I never kept my eyes still for very long. The first few pieces of this book are poems of found poetry, words collected from behind bus windows.

10A Bus Between Chasetown & Brownhills

New dawn chase,
Slow miners rest.
Convenient town hunters,
Greenbelt hospital enterprise.
Burntwood toll,
Stock up now!
Lucius, give way,
Now, for winter.
West Harlequin, East,
You've just passed us.
Buy me Coca-Cola.
Village chippy servicing all makes.
Recovery will be used for prosecution.
Off-licence burgers.
Michelle's memorial heating swift conqueror.
Independent family jigger's whistle
High street metals six a-side.
Next left retribution.
Just eat Wolfe.
Hello shoe research.
Subway flowers for all occasions.
Vegan archers trade emergency divisions.
Rainbows munch frozen babies hands at the Temple
of The Drive Anchor.
Ouch!

X1: Birmingham to Coventry

Sweet and tender sealife,
St Martin's caring for nature.
Magical academy of invention,
Taboo cinema club soft-play nursery open,
Free places for 2 - 4 year olds.

Pause

Kerryman mother clucker,
Clean kilo self storage rhubarb.
Canal fireworks,
Stars,
Dolphin,
Ibis.

Amazing starts here,
No stopping,
Smile alcohol restricted area,
No stopping,
Always.

Beware of cycles,
Freeze your fat,
Clearway we're up and running.
Long partitioning,
St Cyprian's Church private blind spot,
Take care.

Eat here,
Day crèche fried chicken.

Cheaper loco works,
Roaming British,
Healing rays,
Garden of Eden, sold.

The Major boots social warning,
Crematorium overnight,
Blinded by the light.

No more excuses Poundland,
Swan Island news,
Open Wells made easy.
Cityends off licence here,
Traffic queues likely ahead.

Chinese tub,
New rewards,
Vacuum, slow, slow,
No more muddy paws.
Speak to us today,
Mon to Fri from 3pm,
Whiskey to let.

Ice rink savers carvery,
Istanbul Phonegiant dragon.
Yum yum massage and spa,
Complete support services.

The Sun harvester nation's terminal emergency
vehicles cargo,
I turn off when stopped.

Sky chefs,

See something,
Drop off passengers.

Authorised police proceed,
Express smoke,
Say something,
Charge.

In private vehicles Bennetts bring it on,
Come on over,
Two way twisters,
Anti-social Church services.

On the go motorcycle workforce hunters smoke in
this vehicle.

All day breakfasts,
Green zebra,
Bull's head,
Close waterfall,
Dial a triumph.

End of village Hall surgery,
Strawberry fields,
Woodland View,
Park Green,
Pull handle to exit.

Against the law milk,
Sycamore gulf,
For half a mile,
Don't miss our terminus.

Children chilled everyday,
Return your butchers to smoke.

End.
End.
End.
End.

Jacobean estates,
Holy hand car wash,
Summer's not difficult,
Except cycles.

Brothers free Jesus,
60 years young,
Start your electric adventures St John.

X51 :Cannock to Walsall

Superior holiday elegance shore,
Cross Paul sunny field free camera mini autumn
avoiding porcelain ladies,
Only diverted factor 50 covered ends.
Tail backs or bar snacks, man!
Meadow campervan chariot for sale,
Saddle repairs chase florist.
Dazzling dogs bite when only the best will do,
Quiz night Cash welcome.
To your home ground boot and son.
Ramp ahead Marshall oasis,
Bus stop sold.
Disabled people patrol poplar road.
We the spindles you shop dog.
Rescue station Nisa local.
Unloading zone ends alpha way style.
Valeting lamb express.
Keepers cut & packed.
Newtown elderly people entertainment,
Drink filling station.
The lakes ivy House,
Red route warning.
Cemetery litter in Bloxwich,
Stoney bell zero tolerance.
Strawberry montage,
Cheap nail bar stand.
Grill Jeneve oriental harvest parts worn.
Amazing emporium active living,
Still love angels fencing.
Ask the copperfish rascals.

Swift hot chilli coronation beauty.
BoozeLand stitch in time.
Top quality pigeon twenty-five.
Electrical lenders.
College courses for steel.
Clean webbs slow forest.
Primary house loading.
Council seashell jockey made of cars.
Radio religion refreshingly bold worship,
Food hut end of public bar,
His grace stores short funeral directors.
Organic dojo peppermill music

Autofill

I love the autofill buttons on smart devices, those three little buttons that pop up above your keyboard and try to guess what you're going to say. Continuing with the 'found poetry' theme I thought I would experiment with those three buttons and see what came out. All I have done is add punctuation and paragraphs and tried to make some kind of poetic sense out of the jumble but there are some verses that I think are truly magnificent and it's definitely a writing exercise you should try if you're stuck in a rut at any time.

Autofillia

A little girl's in the snow.
The baby boy was found on the edge of the forest.
A heavy winter brings a lot of faith.
The youth had long,
Dyed black hair,
Worn thick.
A heavy heart and mind was a good friend of mine
but I know what I heard from her in the snow last
night.
She is a reading,
A flash of joy with the sun on her face,
But her eyes will fall inside a brightly illuminated
room.

Go check the room,
The bed is a deft one.
It's like a witch,
I don't want to hear anything about your feelings,
Or thoughts on how things go with the wolves.

The Divine Word of God is an absolute blessing to
me and I will never forget about the Lord as he is a
good friend of mine.
He will not fade.

The pangs of my father who fought in the Second
World War were very sad because they were buried
in the first place.
They didn't even have a clue.
Go check out and see what they say;

"I need people to help me with the wolves, too.
I will watch as I am aiming at the end of the world.
What do you know about the situation?
We are now in a position to offer a full service for all
of our countdown prisoners unless you look the
same as the semen flow?"

The little one is the biggest part of the story's plot.
It is a prolific goddess who dips her mandibles into
many genres.
The cure for her 40th birthday will be the first thing I
saw in her last night,
I saw a purple haired Wolverine,
A prolific writer of all things yucky.

Evil is here and I have to walk.
So no more in honour of my favourite people.
I'm in no way professional and friendly.

If we can find a way to help with the Other Side then
please feel free to contact,
We can exchange gifts.

The Little Exorcist is her best bet for a few hours.
You have a superb range of options for your baby on
the streets.
Mixed with wolves,
The people tell you things like a witch hunt.

They say that you can whisper secrets into a true
smile.
Your love is always the way.

You will never know what you can find here in a
cloud of joy.
You may want to write a story inspired by your own
ideas or suggestions,
You can.

After the wedding you will never be seen.
Go check your eyes with a button,
If you press that button,
Out will they will pop.

Hell is a relatively new adoptive.

We were very lucky to have a different place where
we were young and loved.
The doors of our early stages are quite long and very
often we don't want to waste any more time on our
bookshelves.
I think we should put a note in the diary to make
sure we can get the tickets.
We will also need the full details of the stuff I have
written in my pants.

I will watch the rest of this week so I won't be able to
participate.

Autofillia 2

Rotting and I will not be able to walk away from the void.
She has numerous issues,
There is nothing to be done I'm afraid.
I've never been able to participate in stuff,
We were talking about American people who were really keen on taking out the flames devouring him by rolling.
Out the talented team at work!
The last couple was a bright girl who is possessed with a story about real love and her amazing wife who loves her.
Weird fiction is a good thing for all of us who have fallen through the processes of being cut.

On the way back from her side I've seen her in the kitchen like a cat,
I'm afraid she will not be able to help me without further care,
She is a very generous and caring person who will not fade away,
I love her name a little more than she wants,
Poisoning her love for the first time,
I'm not spoiling the fun of one night in a cloud of her mind.
She is an idiot,
A lot of people in her life now have to wait for her to come back,
I have to walk away from her so she will not be able to do it again.

She is just so sick.
She is so much happier now than I expected,
She is just so busy but I will try to get the rest,
I will wait for her,
To come round again.

Little girl has just come back from a haunted night,
The nightmares it's installed will take days to come
down from.

Roads to airport and flight to France,
The first expensive holiday we will not be taking,
We have a deadline for our black hearts,
The end of the day,
Maybe we will be joining,
In a box,
In the garden.

Stuff the best possible chances,
You will find that you will never miss the chance to
breathe,
Your love and your baby will always be on your feet,
You will never miss your chance.
Baby near death in your heart,
With your home,
Family will be forever loved and blessed,
A story inspired you to be young,
A perfect companion,
A haunted smile,
To occasion with the wonderful,
You love a little spotlight,
Spectral wishes shall be yours to grant.

(12 feet of Bridge Street, Walsall)[2]

1.
Let's brew,
Exchange,
Weekly general waste.

2.
Half price,
Strawberry lifelines,
Freshly picked spirits.

---

[2] You can collect/make found poetry even when
walking

(Along the Birmingham Road, Perry Barr)

1.
Bounce merchants crematorium,
Swift collector here,
Angel car park,
One stop Judy.

2.
Taste the dark, Mason Young,
Don't lose the picture,
£2 per day,
Expected legacy.

Funny Stuff[3]

He's A Totally Hardcore Blackbird[4]

He's a totally hardcore blackbird
Always there with the dawn's first word
He's a totally hardcore blackbird
His brains were scrambled in his head
He's a totally hardcore blackbird
Before he bashed out of his egg
He's a totally hardcore blackbird
His mum didn't raise him on regurgitated food
He's a totally hardcore blackbird
Just fed him his siblings after they'd been stewed
He's a totally hardcore blackbird
He sharpened his beak on his parents' bones
He's a totally hardcore blackbird
He kicks grown cuckoos from their homes
He's a totally hardcore blackbird
He steals all of the magpies' sparklies
He's a totally hardcore blackbird
He colours swans in using Sharpies
He's a totally hardcore blackbird
He beats up owls and dates flamingos pretty
He's a totally hardcore blackbird
He killed Keith Harris and left Orville shitty
He's a totally hardcore blackbird
He doesn't have Facebook and he doesn't have
Twitter
He's a totally hardcore blackbird

[4] Inspired by seeing a dead blackbird lying next to a litre bottle of vodka and a syringe the morning after I discovered John Cooper Clarke

He won't go to rehab cuz he ain't no quitter
He's a totally hardcore blackbird
A rolled up joint spraffing out of his beak
He's a totally hardcore blackbird
He'll stone the crows and mock the weak
He's a totally hardcore blackbird
Drinks bottles of vodka bigger than him
He's a totally hardcore blackbird
He wing-wrestled a seagull kicked its quim
He's a totally hardcore blackbird
He once raped Rodan from Godzilla
He's a totally hardcore blackbird
The Big Bang was loud but this bird's shriller
He's a totally hardcore blackbird
He once shagged Big Bird's mum
He's a totally hardcore blackbird
He stuffed Emu up Rod Hull's dead bum
He's a totally hardcore blackbird
He lights his fags on the Phoenix's fire
He's a totally hardcore blackbird
He raced an ostrich and his times were higher
He's a totally hardcore blackbird
A syringe of shit injected in one eye
He's a totally hardcore blackbird
He'll show all the other cunts how to fly
He's a totally hardcore blackbird
The gutter's the place in which he'll die
He's a totally hardcore blackbird
He wants to be immortalised in song
He's a totally hardcore blackbird
A legend to pass down to your young
He's a totally hardcore blackbird
His spectral beak taps at my door

He's a totally hardcore blackbird
He's why The Raven quoth 'Nevermore'
He's a totally hardcore blackbird
You know that Hymn 'Morning Has Broken?'
He's a totally hardcore blackbird
Well, who do you think was the blackbird that had spoken?
He's a totally hardcore blackbird
He pecks these words out inside my head
He's a totally hardcore blackbird
A perverse eternal dawn chorus of the living dead
He's a totally hardcore blackbird
He's made a nest box in my skull
He's a totally hardcore blackbird
He was the iceberg that pierced Titanic's Hull
He's a totally hardcore blackbird
He's the real reason the Dodo don't see the light of day
He's a totally hardcore blackbird
He frightened all the thunderbirds away
He's a totally hardcore blackbird
He taught Eric Draven 'it can't rain all the time.'
He's a totally hardcore blackbird
Now he perches on Satan's shoulder amongst the bird shit and the grime
He's a totally hardcore blackbird
TWEET!

Seasons On The Run

Goodbye to you, my crusted friend,
We've known each other since the flu began,
Together we climbed hills and trees,
Learned of living dead zombies,
They skinned our pets and families.

Goodbye, my friend, it's hard to die,
When you know I'll not have the time to cry,
Now that the virus is in the air,
Pretty girls are everywhere,
They're blue and dead but I don't care.

We had joy, we had fun,
We had seasons on the run,
But the hills that we climbed,
Were just mounds of rotting slime.

Goodbye Papa, please pray for me,
I was the black sheep of the family,
You tried to teach me, keep me in tune,
Mother shagged the milkman, he made her swoon,
That's why you're infected and I'm immune.

Goodbye Papa, you're beyond belief,
The first zombie I've seen with false teeth,
It's a pity you left them in that glass,
Now quit gnawing at my arse,
As a living cadaver you're a farce.

We had joy, we had fun,

We had seasons on the run,
But my mum and my Dad,
Like the seasons,
Have all gone bad.

We had joy, we had fun,
We had seasons on the run,
But you pair got bit like two twats,
It's the reason,
You have both gone bats.

Goodbye Michelle, my lovely wife
I hope your skull is weaker than this knife,
And every time that I was down,
You would always come around,
But now you're mewling on the ground.

Goodbye Michelle it's time to die,
Your fatal head wound's dripping in your eye,
Now that the summer bug is done,
There are walking dead folk grab your gun,
Now the Summer bug has won.
We had joy we had fun,
We had seasons on the run,
To the zombies from whom we were chased,
We were nowt but meat paste.

We had joy, we had fun,
We had reasons which to run,
But the meat you ate weren't duck,
And now you're dead you stupid fuck.

We had joy, we had fun,
We had seasons in the sun,
But our house on the beach,
Like your immune system,
Has been breached.

All our lives we had fun,
We had seasons in the sun,
But the door that was secure,
Is now broken by you,
You stupid whore.

We had joy, we had fun,
We had seasons in the sun,
But now the zombies are inside,
I'm their dinner, "open wide!"

Colleen

Co-leen, Co-leen, Co-leen, Co-leen,
Please don't go Annie Wilkes on my arse,
Co-leen, Co-leen, Co-leen, Co-leen
Please don't take me just because I'm class,
My writing is beyond compare,
With enviable artistic flair,
And my descriptions of gore and horror are the best
you've ever seen,
My prose chills you to the core
And tingles places no one else could explore,
And I understand your fixation with me, Co-leen.
But please don't abduct me,
Take my kids, they're nowt but trash,
Take the wife and porno stash,
Just don't hobble me or keep me your sexual
prisoner, Co-leen.

And I can easily understand
How you think I'm the best author in the land,
But my books aren't really THAT good, Co-leen.
Co-leen, Co-leen, Co-leen, Co-leen,
Please don't go Annie Wilkes on my arse,
Co-leen, Co-leen, Co-leen, Co-leen
Please don't take me just because I'm class.

You could have your choice of books
But few authors have better looks
But I'll not be your sex-slave, Co-leen
I had to have this talk with you
My happiness depends on you

And whatever you decide to do, Co-leen
Co-leen, Co-leen, Co-leen, Co-leen,
Please don't go Annie Wilkes on my arse,
Co-leen, Co-leen, Co-leen, Co-leen
Please don't take me just because I'm class.

Cuppa Tea No. 3

Oh, cup of tea number three,
Will you be the one for me?
To wake me from this half-sleep slumber,
And stop my brain from slipping under?
If you don't what should I do?
Maybe pluck a pube or two?
Or burn myself whilst making toast,
To keep me from giving up the ghost.
Maybe I should go back to bed,
Let CBeebies look after the kids instead?
But no I'll sit here writing this crap poem,
And watch cats and kids destroy my home

H. A. P. P. Y Positive[5]

Coming home covered in grass,
Sun scorched skin and memories to last.
You can find tranquility in the midst of insanity,
A green land oasis in each and every city.
That's where I long to be, positively.

Happiness is free if you want to let it in,
Cast away worries and raise up that chin.
Treat yourself better, listen to the memes,
Your body is a temple, fill it to the seams,
With light and love and everything that's good,
And soon you will start feeling how you should.

Force yourself to sing,
No matter what your voice,
Give away something,
Whatever be your choice,
A gift, a hug, a gesture but purely out of the blue,
Will make the one you give it feel as good as you.

Remember what that geezer said,

---

[5] For some mad reason, maybe too many people had told me I was a miserable bastard, or perhaps I had had sex, I wrote a happy poem, very unlike me. I posted it on Facebook, very like me, and someone, I think it was Al Barz, moaned that it was uncharacteristically happy and that it scared him. What follows this poem is an antidote poem for those who may experience similar symptoms as Al.

The one serene in orange robe,
Live for every moment of life's erratic strobe,
Think about the present,
Be the gift that God sent,
And let it spread like wildfire,
Happiness is an airborne infection,
Share and love and you'll find self-perfection

F.U.C.K Positive[6]

Coming home covered in grass,
Smelling of dog piss bleeding from broken glass.
You can find tranquility in the midst of insanity,
If you gouge out your eardrums to stop the
profanity.
That's where I long to be, positively.

Happiness costs and involves degradation and sin,
Cast away clothes and raise up that chin.
Beat yourself better, listen to the screams,
Your body is a temple, fill it to the seams,
With liquor and hate and everything that hurts,
And soon you will stop feeling when the blood
spurts.

Force yourself to swing,
No matter whether you're clean,
Give away something,
Riddled and obscene,
A punch, a shrug, a gesture borne purely out of
malice,
Destroy the ones you loathe with your aged rotten
phallus.

Remember what that geezer said,
The one dressed like a clown,
Ruin every moment happiness will drown,
Think about the present,

---

[6] The antidote

Abolish all that's pleasant,
And let it spread like wildfire,
Happiness is an airborne infection,
Hatred is the cure, vaccine,
the way to self-perfection

Bored

I'm bored,
I'm chairman of the board.
No, wait that's been done,
I'll start again with another one.
Don't you just hate those pockets of time,
Those inbetweeny bits that slop like slime?
Too late for something,
Too early for that.
Boredom in its purest form,
Suffocates and keeps us warm,
But prevents us from allowing the norm,
Of the everyday hobbies that save us from yawn.
Frozen in time,
Suspended animation but awake,
Clock watching time wasted,
I psychologically ache.

I'm a big Ian Dury fan.
What follows are some tributes to the great man

Wake Up & Make Grub For Me

You come awake,
Beside the gift for womankind,
I'm still asleep,
Now get off your behind.
Rise on this occasion,
Get off of your crack,
Slide down my bannister,
The kitchen's in the back.
The bread is sun-blest,
Oh, please disturb my rest,
I love the smell of bacon in the morning,
Use the whole pack for the best.

Wake up and make grub for me,
Wake up and make grub,
Wake up and make grub for me,
I don't wanna make you,
I'll let the fancy take you,
And you'll wake up and make grub.

I come awake,
In a hungry morning mood,
My stomach makes a naughty niggle,
And let's out noises loud and rude.
Press it against my tummy,
I hope the egg's still runny,
What happens next is private,
It's also very messy.

Don't go giving up the ghost,

Tomorrow I'll make you tea and toast,
But you gotta earn your keep luv,
Cuz I'm great that's not a boast.
So,

Wake up and make grub for me,
Wake up and make grub,
Wake up and make grub for me,
I don't wanna make you,
I'll let the fancy take you,
And you'll wake up and make grub,
Wake up and make grub for me,
Wake up and make grub,
Wake up and make grub for me,
Wake up and make grub,
Wake up,
Wake up,
Wake up,
Wake up.

Reasons To Be Fearful

Why won't these thoughts vacate my head?
Why won't these thoughts stay in my head?
Why won't these farts stay in my bed?
Why don't they stop The Walking Dead?
Why does my stomach feel like lead?
Why do these nights fill me with dread?
Why can't I keep my bank well-fed?
Why can't I get fit drinking Guinness instead?
Why can't I overdose on bread?
Why won't you read the shit I've said?
Reasons to be fearful by me.
1,2,3

Winter slipping dangers, swearing at strangers,
Public no-brainers and snow.
Cold breaking bones, old aching moans,
Heating up our homes no dough.

Eating Al fresco, shopping out in Tesco,
Wasps in my fucking pesto and bugs.
Barometric pressure, the air not being fresher,
Going out on drinking session and hugs.

Gigs in the city, feeling very shitty,
Not feeling very pretty, 'Oh bugger!'
Music's not gelling, me, I'm smelling,
Guinness inside swelling, 'Hi, Mugger!'

Being drunk at bus stops, puking til I can't stops,
Missing out on britpops, why?

Mugger throwing gang signs, me returning
backward peace signs,
Feeling very real, fine, 'bye.'
Reasons to be fearful by me
Reasons to be fearful by me
Reasons to be fearful by me
1,2,3
Reasons to be fearful by me.

People being twatty,
No fun time for Matty,
Watching daytime soaps.
Trying to eat healthy,
Trying to be wealthy,
Accidental gropes.
Chavs and thick inebriation,
The snowflake generation,
Open mic nights.
People dying,
People spying,
Facebook dislikes.
Big gym fails,
Crawling like Snails,
Blubber like whales.
Being a writer,
Stuff's getting shiter,
Sufferin' Kindle sales.
Reasons to be fearful by me.

Going on for an age,
Just to fill another page,
Running out of sage.
Reading this poem,

Wanting to go home,
Switching off me phone.

Going on for too longs,
Saying something too wrongs,
Wondering if this line pongs.

Not knowing when to quit,
Continuing with this shit,
Being a stubborn git.
Pissing off you lot,
Gonna get myself shot,
Now I've had enough of it.
Reasons to be fearful by me.

Ode To A Hypochondriac

What's this pain in my head?
Is it something undetected?
Is this spot on my leg,
Malignantly infected?
What's this twinge in my chest,
Some fat blocking up an artery?
Or just indigestion,
From something cheese and tomaterry?
I've got pains in my elbows,
Up and down my back,
Life ain't easy for a Hypochondriac .
Send me to the doctor's,
And I'll feel fine,
They'll tell me nothing's wrong,
Stop wasting their time.
When I leave the surgery my ailments will be
waiting,
If I check my bollocks anymore,
They're gonna need castrating!
I've got itches in my britches,
And my jaw's gone slack.
Oh I how I hate being a Hypochondriac!

Ode To an RSPCA Street Person[7]

Oh, Miss RSPCA, how you do you flatter?
Say complimentary things it really doesn't matter.
Did I really earn that stare?
Do you really like my hair?
Do you really think I'm cool?
Do you really, really care?
No, you don't, I can't agree that It's funny,
You only say these things, because you want my money!
Down with dog biting,
Down with dog fighting,
I'll give you my bank details, here start writing.
You need money for pets that are sick,
I dig that concept, get your trick.
£1.46 a week may not sound much to you,
But I've got critters that need feed too.
I wish I had the money to help labradors with cancer,
But I don't so please take, 'FUCK OFF!' as my answer!

---

[7] The last of my Ian Dury inspired poems...for now

Shit Poem

I thought I'd write an improv poem,
Whilst sitting on the bog,
Not in the luxury of my home,
I'm in the gym passing this log.
I've eaten too many nuts,
And protein bars this weekend,
God knows what hell,
From my rectum will descend.
The man in the cubicle next,
Swears before he's even locked the door,
The smell of this baby,
Is like the fallout from a nuclear war.
Monday morning and I'm writing rhymes about shite,
If you ask my opinion,
That's how to start the week right.
Now before I stand up and duly inspect,
Upon this conundrum I shall now reflect.
Do I end here on this verse,
Or tell you what my poo looks like,
In details descriptive and perverse?

Sweary Poem

There are things in the world that upset Mankind,
And some are quite rightfully so,
Then there are things that upset,
And I think quite rightfully no.
People get ill-mannered, irate,
Run verbally amok,
When they hear me say things like;
Cunt-flaps, wank-socks, fuck-nuts and COCK
But these are just words dear,
Harmlessly describing,
Anatomical parts, masturbatory accessories....
And whatever 'fuck-nuts are describing.
We use words much more harsh in every day banter,
An example will follow,
Pay attention whilst I canter.

I could murder a cup of tea,
I'll bloody kill my kids for doing that!
I wish I was dead
I wish you were dead
He stabbed me in the back
This place looks like a bomb's gone off,
Why are there orphans and widows with their limbs
blown off?

We all use phrases lightly that mean things far worse
than swears,
So next time you're thirsty why not catch them
unawares?
I could so fuck a cup of tea,

I'll bloody twat my kids for doing that!
I wish I was wanking
I wish you were wanking
I wish we were all wanking!

Why do we get offended at words that mean sex and
body parts?
And use worse words more frivolously than Donald
Trump gets through tarts?
With that I'd like to leave you with a bunch of
improv swearing,
If you want to leave now please do,
It won't be me who's caring.

Wanky-bollocks, shit-bottles,
Double-barrelled's worth a try,
Jesus wanked the fucking bed off!
Nonsensical is my guy,
Fuck my aunt!
That one was thanks to autocorrect,
As well as ducking aunt.
But my favourite swear of all
Has to be cunt.
Said in different accents it's the one word that still
upsets,
Sets people's teeth on edges,
Makes their pants so wet.
So this one is for you,
You cunt haters out there,
I'm going to cure your cuntness,
By saying it until you just don't care.

Cunt, cunt, cunt,

Cunting, cunty, cunts,
Cunt off you cunting cuntbag
Your cunt's on back to front.
Cunt the wall you cunthead,
Your cunt's on sideways, Prick,
Suck my cunt, Cuntwad,
You are a cunting dick.

The Most Beautiful Poem

I want to write something beautiful,
To make people laugh and cry,
Something to be remembered for,
For when I finally die.

I want it to have long words,
With precise poetic form,
I want it to be bold and brass,
Something's that outspoken, iconoclast.
Full of words that make me sound like an
intellectual,
Botanical! Perpendicular! Metrosexual!

It has to unite nations,
Bring an end to war,
Abolish disease and famine, and religious abhor.
Stop death in its Ever-lasting, relentless tracks,
Block flamboyant snowflakes having fanny attacks.

It needs to be transcribed in all languages,
Written in the stars,
Etched onto satellites,
From Pluto back to Mars.

But I'm not built for such a task,
A foolish clown am I,
My jokes as stinking,
As the mud in Peppa's sty.

My poetry is never serious,

I'm all talk, all front,
Beautiful prose escapes me,
I am a silly cunt.

How The Cheshire Cat Lost His Penis

Allow me to introduce myself,
Matty-Bob gifted visionary,
Master of medicine and vicarious veterinary.
Delectable doctor of all and sundry,
Precise practitioner of this Land so wondery.
But enough of my titles, grades and qualifications,
This is a tale of a cat told through poetic recitations.
An extraordinary feline they call the Cheshire Cat,
A vanishing cat a magic cat,
Well fancy that.
Not the story of the Space-Hog from the mounds of
Venus,
This is the tale of How The Cheshire Cat Lost His
Penis.

It was a long time ago on a day quite calm,
I was working away on a visibility balm,
The Queen of Hearts deemed it my duty,
To create a cream to enhance her beauty.
As ever my house was filled to the brim,
With inhabitants of Wonderland and the states they
were in.
The gryphon with beak-rot,
The Dodo with gout,
The Walrus with tusk wounds,
After larking about.
But ahead of these creatures came a case quite
extreme,
Ghastly, ungodly, I held back a scream.

A nightmarish vision,
A basket of bone,
Pulsating red organs,
A perpetual moan.
Fur on the inside,
On the outside a network of vein,
"Why," I cried, "Chesh friend, you've fucked up
again!"
For at once I noticed that this barrel of gore,
Was my old friend the Cheshire,
At he let out a roar.

Now this you might know,
This you might not,
But my friend the Cheshire Cat can vanish a lot.
His gift of disappearing and materialisation,
Is famous throughout Our Majesty's nation.
But sometimes this old fluff box,
Causes himself quite a flummox,
With his head on backwards,
Or his paws on his bollocks.
You see my old friend was fond of fishing for
rainbow bright trout,
Splashing through the river and yanking them out.
But these fishes were poisonous to this particular
feline,
Even though he knew this would lead him to mine.

It was obvious that a problem had occurred,
When he tried reappearing the result was absurd.
He was inside out,
He was outside in,
Skeleton on the outside,

Squishy within.

I understood his condition,
Knew what to do,
"I'll have you right moggy,
Just see that I do!"
I rolled up a sleeve and warmed up one hand,
And thrust my thumb vigorously against his anal
gland.
A vaporous cloud of green gases so vile,
Erupted from Chesh Cat making me smile.
With a flicker and blink,
With a flutter and flash,
The kitty switched off,
And back on with a crash.
There he stood tail up and proud,
He smiled and purred but then howled aloud.
"My friend what's the matter?
Are you still sick?"
"No," said the Cheshire,
"But where is my dick?"
I tried not to laugh,
Though he looked so forlorn,
But I found this amusing,
The Cat with no horn.

This talk of phallus,
Brought to mind of Alice,
And what she did chat,
"I've seen a cat without a grin,
But not a grin without a cat."
It's funny to think this animal can vanish at will,
Not just parts of him,

But whole bits as well,
Headless or limbless,
In the shape of a sock,
So how comes this kitty,
Has misplaced his cock?

I stroked him and offered a comforting song,
I reassured the Cheshire Cat that I'd find his schlong.
I asked him where he had seen it last,
He tensed and thrashed his tail,
When he had lunch with the Queen of Hearts,
I started to run pale.
The Queen of Hearts had been gifted,
A poodle rare and pink,
The dainty dog had chased the cat,
It was worse than I would think.
The Cheshire Cat was not one to fall at the jaws of
some gay doggy,
The Cheshire Cat had lured the dog to pastures dark
and foggy.
He smiled at me the cat he did,
Grin evil and malicious,
"I raped that dog, ripped out his throat,
And left him for the fishes."
"But Cat you see,"
Said I to he,
"The error of your slaughter,
You fucked the dog,
But left your cock,
And now it's in the water!"

Cheshire's face fell,
His whiskers lank and droopy,

The thought of his dear penis,
Sinking down through something gloopy.
You see as amazing as he was it left him quite
distraught,
How he could vanish parts of him but never teleport.
A freak mistake,
A moment of dog-related Lust,
Saw this poor cat without a dick,
His Penis he had bust.

The Cheshire Cat left my place mournful and sadly,
An encounter such as his may end even more badly.
The Queen of Hearts loves her pets,
And now she will see red,
This mangy cat,
This stupid twat,
Will have a bounty on his head.
A low profile the cat will keep,
From now on I do predict,
He'll hide away all night and day,
Keep his appearances strict.
Although I tell you this,
Your laughter's quite a racket,
For well you know that missing dick,
Is hidden in my jacket.

Mack The Slipper

He had scoured the earth for books on killers,
From genuine biographies to armchair thrillers.
Mack was obsessed with the bringing of death,
It started long ago with his only friend Geoff.
The first time he smacked him and saw the coming of
red,
Was the time violence whacked him and filled his
head.
He killed him too quickly though but somehow got
away,
It would be ten years before again he went astray.

During that hiatus Mack read up on murderous
sages,
There was only one kind that were remembered
through the ages.
Serial killers of more than three or five,
No failed attacks, no one left alive.
He wanted to be famous for his kills,
Wanted his name to induce spinal chills.
He swatted up on books about Gacy, Fish and
Crippen,
Studied evidence about Jack when he was ripping.
He needed an angle, a trend or gimmick
Most of them had them, something to inspire not
mimic.
Some ate their victims, acts of cannibalistic
suggestion,
But that would probably turn his guts, give him acid
indigestion.

Some liked to strangle, butcher, dismember and molest,
But that sounded quite icky and something he might detest.
Even though the urge to kill was relentless, never stopping,
The last thing Mack wanted was to end the fun mopping.

So he thought about this and he thought about that,
Thought about practicing on a doggy or a cat.
But he rather liked animals and those in stress got him riled,
So he considered the possibility of killing a child.
But kids were cute, apart from Geoff who was a wanker,
And all he done to him was hit him and tie him to an anchor.
Mack thought about people and the types that got his goat,
Old grumpy people, miserable scrotes.

Enough planning, enough of fantasy,
Mack brought his lusts out into reality.
Merryweather Retirement Home was the place where he would hit,
And in particular one certain cantankerous old git.
He used to be his teacher back at primary school,
Telling him off, making him a fool.
But now he was decrepit and sitting in the home,
Waiting for Death to select his name from his never ending tome.

He dug the hole discreetly out back behind a hedge,
And snuck into the home and into a closet he did wedge.
When the old cunt fell asleep, snoring beyond belief,
Mack picked him up, as light as a leaf.
Outside he did take him and into the hole he went,
Mack then regretted the time that he had spent.
The hole was too shallow or the old teacher too tall,
No matter how he tried he couldn't bury him all.
So instead of digging deeper like any decent killer would,
Mack thought he could work with it, everything was good.
He buried him headfirst during rain and wind and sleet,
And chuckled to himself at the old man's protruding slippered feet.
An accidental gimmick that had a funny quirk,
They'd call him Mack The Slipper, this could work.

Over the months a string of deaths ensued,
Mack felt content, a happy little dude.
But then one day he noticed a rising fashion,
A drop in slipper usage, they were dampeners of passion.
But Mack would not be beaten, not be deterred,
Even though his plans turned out more absurd.
He would buy slippers in bulk, of a tartan finish,
And this is where poor Mack's luck began to diminish.
You see a rise in slippered corpses made old folk despair,

They threw their slippers out, burned them without care.
Mack brought his own slippers to place on the feet of dead,
He thought he was being clever but he was misled.
A paper trail started leading back to him,
His bank account agreed and that reasoned why it was so slim.
The police caught him during his breakfast of kipper,
But he was chuffed, the day's newspaper made him chipper,
Not only had he beaten the one they called The Ripper,
But the reporter had heralded him 'Mack The Slipper.'

Serious Stuff

Black Blood

Forever must I crawl through the sodden fetid faeces
of this mortal coil?
The desire to lance this puss-filled rancid boil that
the happy call 'life'.
I want to end it in a flash of burning pain,
And from my wrists the ebb of blood shall drain.
To end this suffering, kept in this pit of melancholy
hopelessness
To cease this gangrenous putrid existence once and
for all.
Free myself from the things that I am,
The things that I do,
The things that I allow.
To sever my ties with this continuation,
My isolation,
Loneliness beyond restoration,
Hatred beyond redemption.
I want to dissolve the ties that bind me here,
Their coiled malevolence like barbed wire.
And feel ultimate release as all my life,
All my energy,
All my thought,
All my hurt,
All my depravation,
Surges out of my tortured, scarred unclean body.

Autism Rocks

Autism rocks
They weigh me down
Bound around my neck
Hung over my head
In a thick hessian sack
Where they clatter and crash
And bash at my soul
My heart and my will
Inciting thoughts of suicide and worse
Autism rocks

Autism rocks
Chained to my ankles
Concreted boots
Drowning slowly
Suffocating but never enough to destroy
Autism rocks

Autism rocks
Gargantuan boulders obstructing all exits
Controlling everything I do
Always one step ahead
Always there with a trump card to play
Always there to ruin my day
A frequency almost always out of tune
Fleeting moments of synchrony before more crazy
static.
Autism rocks

Autism rocks

And when it's in a good way
The guilt resides for the bad things that it made you
wish
The hatred
The evil
The bitter
The selfish
Autism rocks

Last Night I Said "I Love You," As Usual

Last night I said "I love you," as usual,
I expected her answer, as usual,
It came slightly delayed, unusual,
The flu had debilitated her despite my refusal.
Yesterday she said she wished she were dead,
This was nothing new, a catchphrase re-said,
As she lay on the sofa-made bed.
This morning she laid in, a usual thing,
Saved for weekends or Bank Holiday morning.
I took her a mug and expected a hug,
But she was comatose, not even a shrug.
I placed the tea down on the cupboard beside,
Not realising then that my mother had died.
Although this was worse, just partial physical death,
Who knows what was inside still taking a breath,
Stroke is too nice a word for this evil conjunction,
Death's black velvet glove coaxing malfunction.
Paralysed from the neck down,
Shut up inside, inwardly drown,
I prayed for her death from day one to day seven,
And then thank you God she took the expressway to
Heaven.

Little Zombie Poem

I love you little zombie,
Nothing can beat,
The look of satisfaction,
Every time you eat.
Although you never notice me,
I've watched you from afar,
From behind the rusting fences,
And underneath the burnt out car.

I love you little zombie,
Although I mourn your vacant stare,
And the way you're getting greener,
And the shedding of your hair.
I wish you'd been alive,
When I'd first seen your eyes,
Bloodshot blue and matt look, and permanent
surprise.

I love you little zombie,
We really have to meet,
I don't mind if you consume me,
Just don't start at my feet.
Make it quick and painless,
Quickly through and through,
I don't mind being eaten,
By one as beautiful as you.

I love you little zombie,
In heaven or in hell,
I hope we end up together,

And our stories we may tell.

Make Waves

Make waves in the tranquil ocean,
Scream loud enough to make snow fall from the
highest mountain.
Bury your head in the biggest desert,
Keep turning the other cheek until you break your
neck.
Tune your mind into the unknown frequencies,
Listen to the quietest of voices.
Ignore the facts until they become lies,
Tug the wool over your eyes until you are blind.
Fight against the demons within,
They are you so you can win.
Do not ignore the things that you harmlessly crave,
For the choice won't be there when you're in the
grave.
Dying
Lying
Spying
Defying
Victory comes to you the moment you stop!

Mr. Hide[8]

Constantly running from that fella within,
The dastardly deviant tempter of sin.
He whispers quietly from the space behind my head,
Promising this is the last time that he'll need to be
fed.
One muttered sentence is all that it takes,
For so few words so many mistakes.
A deluge of gluttony, a widening crack,
Endless debauchery, all sealed by his pact.
Mr Hide beckons, persuades and he wins,
The dastardly deviant tempter of sins.
And here in the aftermath awash with regret,
Self-hatred, repulsion, guilt and the want to forget.
But no sign of the deviant now he's had his way,
Rapacious and wanton my will he doth slay.
He will hide and leave me alone on the ground,
Used and abused beneath my own burial mound.
But he will be back and yes he might win,
This dastardly deviant tempter of sin.

---

[8] Mr. Hide, a deliberate misspelling of Dr Jekyll's Mr
Hyde, is the name I give to the voice within that still
encourages me to have an extra spice of bread, chocolate
etc. He's a prick.

Making Mr Hide

I wondered where he'd gone,
That little voice,
The tempter within,
I didn't think a physical manifestation was possible.
But there he stands,
A five stone midget version of myself,
His skin rough with inflamed infection.
This is my southern fried baby,
The five stones I have lost since May,
Come for revenge.
His skin is slick with boiling fat that seeps from every
pore,
Pastry psoriasis between the wrinkles and rolls.
His tongue a wedge of fatty bacon slapping against
candycorn teeth;
Cackling,
Spitting melted cheese phlegm.
What will become of me when there is nothing left to
give?

Mortistic

Trapped by the one you love
Equal amounts of love and loathing
How can someone whose love makes you quiver,
Ignite anger's shiver,
And make me sadly wither?
Cursed but blessed
A joy but a pest
A life without rest
An impossible test.
I love him, I love him I keep telling myself,
Who else understands him?
Nobody else.
Endless smiles but also endless vex,
Heavenly easy but a hellish complex.
I tune into his frequency and feel like I've won,
But then he switches his signal and I come undone.
Dark thoughts happen at the height of the bad,
My life, his life, our life is mad.
My life's little angel is also a Demon,
The best thing my balls did,
Or a pox on my seen?
He is my sun my moon and my earth,
From the blood-freckled prune that he was at his
birth,
To the miniature me with my height and my girth.

Oh Mortimer, my awkward little sod,
No matter what happens beside you I trod,
No option have I although sometimes I wish that
wasn't true,

As my life isn't life unless it's with you

Rant #5

I hate people
Entitled pricks
Who claim ownership
Over everything
Demand your respect
Demand royalty treatment
For breathing the same air
They get free just like me
For walking down the same paths
Littered with shite and bad memories
Thinking they're better and have right of way
Of anything weaker
Survival of the fittest
Every man for himself.
I'd rather die fighting for every man
Than for myself
The world isn't going to adapt for people who are
different,
The ignorant will always tip the scales

One Night In Digbeth - A True Story

Let me tell you about the time I tried to recapture my
youth,
And unintentionally nearly killed someone.
It was May,
The hot kind that hint we might be getting a decent
Summer after all,
Something rare in itself,
And I had the whole day free from my wife and kids.
I was going to Birmingham to see Echobelly,
A band whom I adored in the late Nineties and
thought the lead singer Sonya was the cutest woman
in the world.
Obviously their money had dried up,
Or they were simply cashing in on the twenty year
anniversary of the heights of Britpop like all the other
bands that were crawling out of the woodwork.
They were performing in a tiny little venue in
Digbeth,
One I had never had the displeasure of going to but I
couldn't miss the opportunity to finally crush on
Sonya,
Even though it was twenty years after I fell in love
with her on Top Of The Pops.
I lazed my way down Digbeth late in the afternoon
with only the vague knowledge of knowing where I
was going.
I passed the coach station which ignited memories,
Mostly good ones, of my first ever glimpses of
England's third city;

Once when I was ten on a coach trip to Colwyn Bay,
And another twelve years later when I finally saw
more of Birmingham than the dark,
Grey interior of a bus garage.

I found the venue,
And got the lay of the land.
Virtually next door to the place where the band
would be playing was a pub called The Kerryman,
its sign bedecked in gold and green reminding me of
Greene King beer,
Which in turn reminded me of my dad.
What better way to pass a few hours than sampling
the Guinness in this apparently Irish themed pub?
I soaked up the atmosphere.
I think I was lucky and got the place on a good day,
Either that or it truly is one of Birmingham's magical,
Hidden places.
Old guys crooned along to songs about the heather,
The rolling hills and the mountain sides.
I could barely understand a word they sang but it
was in tune,
And sung with the passion of one who has seen and
felt what they were singing about.
There was a big,
Beautiful black greyhound called Lady who I
instantly fell in love with.
I cradled her face in my hand when her owner left
her in my charge as he went to the toilets and told
her she had beautiful eyes.
The Guinness was good.
I got very drunk.

I chatted complete and utter nonsense with people I
didn't know and would probably never see again
and then eventually went next door to the Institute to
queue up for the band,
Echobelly,
And to see Sonya,
The crush of my teenage years.
Doors opened at eight,
So I was expecting band on by nine and hopefully
leaving just after eleven at the latest.
By then I had a belly full of Guinness and wanted my
bed.
I had been up a long time and despite reliving some
of my youth unfortunately I couldn't relive the
energy I had back then.
I went to the bar to find out two shocking things;
One,
Pints of Guinness were over five pounds,
And two,
Echobelly weren't due on stage until half past ten!
This upset me.
It was a noisy place and dark.
I felt old, bored and if I was going to be sat in that
place for two and a half hours waiting for the band,
I wanted cheaper drinks and friendly,
Random strangers I could hear when I forced them to
talk to me.
So, I thought,
I know; I'll go back next door..
As I passed the bouncers I told them I would come
back later.
They said I wouldn't be allowed to return once I left.
This angered me,

I had an argument with the doorman and ended up
throwing my ticket at him and shouting,
"I'm not waiting for 3 hours in a rubbish venue just to
fulfil some fantasy over a woman that I fancied
twenty years ago!"
I went back to The Kerryman and drank more
Guinness,
Chatted to my new friends for life and cuddled the
hell out of Lady the greyhound.
The fifteen pounds I wasted on the ticket was worth
the company of those incredible individuals.
About eleven o'clock I felt sick and tired so made my
farewells and left.
I stumbled across the city to find the closest bus stop.
I remember making it to the 51 stand and seeing I
had five minutes to wait,
Which was pretty good timing.
The sickness of a belly full of Guinness and nothing
else churned inside me but I hoped that would pass
before the bus came.
Then out of nowhere a big man grabbed me by my
shirt (I lost a button!) and demanded I give him my
phone and wallet.
Fear and an intense,
Dizzying wave of nausea overcame me and things
went extremely blurry.
The next thing I knew he was on the ground and I
was violently vomiting over his face.
I thought I had killed him.
I looked up.
The bus was coming.
The alluring prospect of my bed was more
important.

I would deal with the repercussions when I was
sober.
I showed the bus driver,
Who was strangely wetting himself laughing,
My ticket and took a seat.
I bravely turned my face to glance out at the murder
scene.
The guy who tried to mug me was wiping chunks of
my puke off his face,
Spitting mouthfuls of brown Guinness gruel,
And flailing his arms about in an angry fashion,
Throwing fists,
Gang-signs and obscenities at the bus as it pulled
away.
I was shocked by it all,
But I didn't feel sick anymore and it made me realise
that some things,
Like my youth,
Teenage crushes,
And scary looking gangsta's faces,
Are better left buried beneath the years and
Guinness-flavoured vomit.

Seaside

The town like the elderly lady is tired and weary but
look closely and beauty is not hard to find
Weathered and battered
Aged and defined
It's youthfulness reaped
It's better years mined
She sees times which aren't there
When she felt full of life
Times when she glowed
Times when she growed
And still she remembers the sights and the sounds
The exterior ages but the foundation's the same
But with years she's forgotten
Just another lost name

The coastal town mimics its patrons,
The glassy eyed windows stare across distance and
time
The sea shaped sand like a man's crinkled brow
Remembering back to those family days
But the town is forgotten like the old man
Yet memory of what once was will remain
Till the sun has scorched the sands last grain

There's always a melancholy atmosphere about
British seaside resorts that intrigues the morbid side
of me.

These places seem to sit and gaze mournfully out
across the water like geriatrics with the happy
family-filled memories of yesteryear still caught in
the reflections of their darkened windows.

Where will you be in a hundred years time?
Seasalted green with corrosion and grime.
But still you sit staring blankly over steel water,
After mankind has shunned you and left you for
slaughter.
Used up your vibrance, vitality and vigor,
And now you're left with senility and death's coming
rigor.
Ten thousand great summers of sunshine and
splendor,
From the earliest of settlers to the last lowly vendor.
One day nature will claim back what was taken,
The shattered facades and memories forsaken,
Until maybe in future your joy reawaken.
Beneath seaweed you'll rot,
Beneath shell and sand,
Beneath the sea when it comes to cover the land,
But will you remember the laughter and cheer,
The endless long summer of yesteryear

THE GHOSTS OF BILL HANSON

It was the night before Halloween,
And all through the mansion,
Stirred walking dead corpses,
And the ghosts of Bill Hanson.
Beneath the floorboards,
Woke rotting dead hordes,
Strangled with ropes,
Wires and cords.
In this decrepit old house,
Slept its most evil owner,
Lived their all his life,
A desperate loner.

Driven to murder,
To feed his perversions,
Strangles then buries,
Beneath two red nasturtiums,
In his lonely old house,
Stuck out in the Styx,
No one found out,
How he got his fix.
So he killed and he killed,
Beneath the floorboards they went,
If he killed anymore,
He'd need a basement.

But still he killed and he killed,
He soon ran out of space,
Bodies hidden all over the place,
Up in the attic,

Under the floors,
Behind the walls,
And behind blocked doors.

But one day,
Not so long ago,
People stopped coming,
Causing him,
A traumatic blow.
He took out his acts,
On stray cats and rats.
Until nothing was left,
And he was alone,
Only he,
Was left in his home.

For months and months,
Awake night after night,
When the voices started,
He was stricken with fright.

And with time they grew louder,
The voices from the mansion.
And he became madder.

Then it was the night,
Called Halloween,
The night that the dead,
Can wake from their dream.
And in the house,
There was a lot of dead,
Whose whispers of vengeance,
Chilled him with dread.

He ran through the house,
Down through the halls,
As decaying dead people,
Burst from the walls.
Down from the attic,
And up through the floors,
From out of locked closets,
And out of blocked doors.
Bill Hanson he fled,
From the rotting corpse swarm,
But there were too many,
In this vengeful dead storm.

They grabbed at his arms,
They grabbed at his legs,
They clawed at his eyes,
And bashed in his head.
They ripped and they bit,
They strangled and tortured,
And planted him beneath the house,
In their evil dead orchard.

Music

Sleep, eat, gym, housework, Dad stuff, music,
Bed time's when I get to lose it.
Collapsing on beds physically exhausted,
My body aches, willingly slaughtered.
This is me time,
Free time,
Sublime.
Headphones on it's how I unwind.
Music soothes me,
An audible balm,
Can induce happiness,
Reinstall calm.
Bring back memories of times long gone,
Things I did right,
Things I did wrong.
Sometimes the memories are changed,
The song is given a new life,
Once loved becomes estranged.
Lisa came in my head whenever I heard the Happy
Mondays,
But now it's that cheeky little git,
Drunken Saturdays and apologetic Sundays.
Sad memories turned to endearing chats,
From idiotic children to lovable twats.
The Cure used to make me wanna die,
But I don't sob at Boys Don't Cry.
Now I just sing and envy him that hair,
And bask in the knowledge that I now no longer
care.
But the good ones still make me laugh,

Like Sunshine Superman and that time in the bath.
Angel Of Death gets me through at the gym,
Praise You and Gangsta Trippin' that housemartin
FatboySlim.
Portishead's Third makes me think of one
worthwhile,
With her Machine Gun Threads and her wicked
Nylon Smile,
Take me back to that summer I'd like to stay there a
while.
Then comes a song immortalised in a film's score,
Don't Fear The Reaper brings Captain Trips to my
door.
Freebird slams the fireflies back in their car,
Bright Eyes brings back frightened childhood rabbit
dreams in blooded fields from a far.

Lost in music,
Surrounded by sound,
Simmering in symphony,
That's where I'm to be found.

The Janitor of Auschwitz

They came in droves,
Out of respect and remorse,
Out of love and honour,
And morbid curiosity, of course.

Some were zombified drones,
Hovering over the place where a million died,
Some seemed unaffected,
Some people cried.

HE could deal with all that,
As HE tidied their mess,
Some hid their feelings,
Some cloaked their distress.
But the ones who took pictures,
Got under HIS skin,
This was a place of death,
A place of sin.
It should not be destroyed,
But ever shown for what passed,
A forced education,
A memorial that lasts.

Instagram teenagers posing,
Beneath arches on tracks,
Where Nazis shepherded families,
With flayed open backs.
Their wounds open wide,
Like cattle and carts,
Trampling over felled loved ones,

Whilst today's teenagers swapped photos for hearts.

It angered Him to see their make-up, laced poses,
Flicking the peace sign,
Like it would undo the gas hoses.
HE heard one one day try and account for their
actions,
An elderly couple confronted their photographic
distractions,
A pompous hipster with beads in his hair,
Spouted about love, compassion and care,
How these places should be filled with happiness
and joy,
Not sadness and sorrow,
For those are all ploy,
To beat the horrific is to remember,
But not show it concern,
To erase all proof that it happened,
Not to mourn and yearn.
The old man paled and held up a shaking finger,
'I'll tell you a story and on this you shall linger,
When I was but six I came out of here alive,
But I shall tell you what happened what I did to
survive,
I buried myself,
Crawled down low and deep,
Beneath a ditch of gassed Jewish mothers in search
for my own,
It was a better way to go than what Hitler would
condone.
I still smell their decaying flesh,
And taste the juices that run from that mess.
But I found my mother's hand and held on to it tight,

I told I loved her,
Bid her one last good night.
And now I come back yearly to think of my mother
and pass my reflection,
And to give my thanks for those corpses' protection.'
The pompous hipster smiled but it was laced with
patronising bore,
He and his group of Instagram hippies had made
their minds up nothing more,
So when the elderly couple left, disgusted,
The Janitor invited them to his midnight tour.

The Janitor of Auschwitz gave them all volunteer
seats,
As he demonstrated on them,
An array of Mengele's treats,
And uploaded their photos on Twitter for tweets.

They Call Me Grandad

They call me Grandad,
Me mates, Joe and Bill,
They look at me funny,
Like I'm crazy or ill.
Say, 'that's not our name,
Don't you know who we are?'
'Course I do, matey, was
Only yesterday we was out in your car.'
Joe looks at me with sorrowful eyes,
Billy's holding back the laughter,
I can see through his disguise.

They take me for a fool,
Having me on,
Always joking Billy,
Joe, and Tom.
'Where's Tom?' Says I,
Looking around,
'last time I saw him,
He was at the fairground.'
'Who's Tom, Grandad?
Who's Billy? Who's Joe?'
'I'M NOT YOUR FUCKING GRANDAD!' I yell,
'Alright, stop having a go.'
The little one, Billy he starts bawling in fits,
'I'm sorry,' I says, 'sorry Bill for shouting like,
But this joke ain't funny, getting on me tits.'
'It's okay, Dad...' Joe starts,
But I shoot him a look,
He knows what that means,

He can read me like a book.
He knows all our tricks whilst out on the street,
The stuff we get up to,
And the people we meet.
That look means Shut it,
You're going too far,
Keep talking that shit,
You'll end up in the boot of me car!

Joe looks uncomfortable,
Down at the box on me lap,
He reaches for it,
But I gives it a tap,
'So what's this then?
A box of beer for the night?'
'We'll open it later,' Joe says,
'The time's not right.'
'Bollocks to that,' I say and reach for the card,
He tries to grab it,
But my grip is a bit hard.
I lift the lid,
And Billy's at it again,
Dunno what's up with him,
We're fucking grown men!
I look into the box,
Into the parcel,
And stare in Joe's face,
And call him an arsehole.
'I'm not eighty-four,
And I'm nobodies father,
And as for a Grandad,
What a fucking palaver!
You're having a laugh,

Taking the piss,
I'm only twenty,
I've had enough of this!'
I push the cake onto the floor,
And get out of me chair,
Me legs feel funny,
So I take extra care.

They're still at it with the Grandad,
Joe's saying Dad, twisting the screws,
God I feel fucked,
Like I've been on the booze.
The room's spinning,
And I feel weak with the flu,
If I didn't know I was actually twenty,
I'd start thinking what they said was true.
My head's spinning,
We must have been on the sauce,
It'll explain all silly buggery,
And feeling weird, of course.
I don't even know where I am,
Ain't been here before,
I see a sign with toilet,
Written on the door.

I go in,
The boys still following behind,
Loyal my lads,
Even though we can all be unkind.
They support me,
I'm their best friend,
Billy and Joe always there for me,
Right up til the end.

Billy's still blubbing,
And I wonder what's giving him gyp,
I look down at the wet patch,
A-spread on my hip.
'Happens to us all Bill,
When we've had too much drink.'
'It's alright, Dad.' Joe says,
As we approach a sink.
In the mirror above,
Stands a tall, dark-haired man,
To the opposite edge,
A carbon copy years younger with a darker tan.

Centrepiece like a weathered old fig,
A headshrinker ornament,
A living cadaver that's danced its last jig.
A thing so haggard it looks barely alive,
A thing so ancient it should be buried in sand,
A thing so old it shouldn't be able to walk on this
land.
A thing aged and decrepit,
Toothless and wrinkled,
Virtually bald and deeply crinkled,
It looks frightened and lost,
Its drenched in its own piss,
When it's gummy mouth speaks,
It's barely a hiss.
A brief glimmer of reality,
I still am who I am,
I cling to my boys,
My son Billy and my grandson Sam.

Trollied - A performance poem for two[9]

(Paul & Matt mime walking. At first they take it in turns to lean towards the mic)

Paul *forlorn*- Grocery shopping on a Friday night,

Matt *happy & excited - Cheer up you old fucker, you'll be alright.

Paul - Melancholy lethargy disabling plight,

Matt - Posh way of saying you're feeling like shite.

Paul - Oh, why oh why did I leave this task 'til last minute?

Matt - Why, oh why cuz you're a lazy arse init?

Paul - Wandering townward in a brain-numbed meander,

Matt *pointing* - Some fit birds over there let's have a gander!

Paul - The beautiful ones pass me no glance as I pass by their back,

Matt *cocking a thumb at Paul*) I told you you look like a nonce in that mac.

Paul - The supermarket doors slice like a butcher's blade chopping,

Matt *rolls eyes* - Fucking hell dude we're only shopping!

Paul *hands shaking* - The list is clammy in my shaking hand my pencil but a nub,

Matt *wanker sign* - Too many bloody hours spent on bloody Pornhub.

---

[9] This was written by me for me and Paul B. Morris. Hopefully one day we'll be able to perform it.

Paul *eyes darting about* - The crowds like a flock of ravenous vulture,
Matt *jumping up and down excitedly, grabbing Paul's arm and pointing* - Ooo, special on Peroni let's get a bit of culture!
Paul *stumbling* - I can not do this I fall against a trolley,
Matt *punches Paul in arm* - Stop taking the piss you stupid bloody wally!
Paul - The walls tower over me aisles becoming more narrow,
Matt *nudges with elbow* - Ey, it's that geezer from the market, that fella with the marrow!
Paul - A familiar face though definitely not one of friend
Matt *linking arms with Paul * - Let's show that silly bastard shit he can not comprehend!
Paul *cowers* - The man who mocked me with a vegetable in the middle of the street,
Matt *bravado* - "Oi you fucking bollock, come over here, shift your feet!"
Paul - No, he's coming over to destroy me again,
Matt *bravado* *takes mic out of stand* - "Alright you pikey arsehole, I'm gonna bash your brain!"

BOTH ON THE FLOOR WITH MICROPHONE - they pass it back and forth
Paul - I'm lying in aisle 1 my nose is ruin,
Matt - Fucking t-shirt looks like the shroud of Turin.
Paul *still on the floor, pointing up at shelf* - I spy the Weetabix on the shelf up above,
Matt *sits up & pulls some obscene gesture* - I spy that woman in the short skirt, "hello love."

Paul- The Weetabix man laughs at me,
he's the man from the market stall,

MATT GETS UP PAUL KEEPS MIC

Matt *says down to Paul* *You're fucking nuts
matey, fucking up the wall!
Paul*huddles in terror* -My enemy retreats I give up
cowering in terror,
Matt *helps Paul up* - "That's it walk away!" *shouts
to invisible man, then to Paul*- that's his bloody
error.
PUT MIC BACK
Paul *mimes grabbing jar off shelf* - Shit, he's
coming back, I grab a jar of Splenda,
Matt *hides behind Paul* - That ain't gonna do nowt
you stupid bloody bender!
Paul - Something flashes in his hand, the glimmer of
a knife,
Matt *fake bravado from behind Paul* - "Come on
you scummy arsehole, I'll take you and your wife!"
Paul *uses mic to mime stabbing in chest therefore
taking it out and falling to the floor* - He punches his
hand forward, something grates against chest bone,
Matt *looking down at Paul - no mic* - Fuck this shit
matey, you're on your own.
Paul *mimes blood spurting from chest and dies* -
I'm dying in aisle 1 bloody gushing from my chest,
Matt *shrugs, bends down and takes mic off Paul and
steps over corpse*
- Don't blame me mate, I did my best.
I'm the voice of your fake bravado,
Of all your stupidest ideas,

I'll ignite and rekindle,
New and forgotten fears.
I'll lead you up the garden path,
And get you in the shit,
And when that faeces hits the fan,
I'll get away with it).
drops mic onto Paul's dead body turns back to crowd.

Paul *dying on the floor* - The cold is crushing over me,
Wave after uneventful wave,
An insignificant death of,
an insignificant knave.
An embarrassment in death,
As well as in life,
Killed in aisle number by a market dweller's knife.
PAUL STANDS UP AND BOTH FACE CROWD TO TREMENDOUS APPLAUSE.

Violence

There's so much fucking violence in this world.
Everywhere I look I see ghosts of what might have
been done,
And what's still yet to come.
Nightmarish scenarios play out before my eyes in an
alternative reality,
That's unfortunately not that unlikely.
It might not happen to me or mine,
But it's out there happening to them, and theirs.
Nothing has changed, the imagery is just far more
accessible.
Social media is a curse and a miracle.
It spreads this infection,
Sometimes glorifying,
Sometimes rectifying.

I saw the old man stabbed the burglar,
His knife was bigger,
Like Crocodile Dundee.
The floral tributes for one who would have stolen
and maybe killed
Crushed and destroyed beneath angry boots.
``no one deserves to die,' said the man's sister,
But how far would her brother had gone to get what
he wanted?

Children stealing bikes off other children
And filming on phones.
Safety in numbers.
Bravado in numbers.

Successfully fucking mugging innocent people in
numbers.

I fear for my children
And what they may be subjected to.
I fear that they will partake in things of this nature.

How do the parents feel?

The ones who really aren't to blame.
The ones who really did try their best.
The ones who really did give their child everything.
The ones who really did bring them up right,
Teach them right from wrong,
When they see their own children,
In a Facebook video,
Beating a school mate to a bloodied pulp,
Stealing a random passer-by's phone,
Taunting someone with special needs,
Or seeing their name on the rain-spattered tag of a
crushed floral tribute,
Outside the house of an eighty-year old man who
was protecting himself and his wife?

A Place I'd Only Heard Of On The Football Fixtures

A place I'd only heard of on the football fixtures,
Whilst waiting for something good to come on,
I never thought that one day I'd ever go there,
I never thought that one day I'd become one.

Penpalling was life for me back then,
A shy reclusive soul trapped in my Suffolk pen,
The same people and routines again and again.
I took the first offer of love that was given,
A lively young lady who I've not long forgiven.

She showed me nightlife,
Culture and change,
Places where people were like me,
Peculiar and strange,
The Trough and The Vault were places where we
became free,
She taught me the pleasure and pains of love,
Sex and alcohol and then she left me be.

I never felt complete until I wandered these streets,
And although some run it down,
It always remained beneath my feet.
Through thickness and thin,
Through marriage and death,
Through birth and rebirth,
Through sadness and mirth.

It feels like home,

I've been here half my life,
Always in the same place,
But now with another wife,
And two little terrors,
Who I often wish could grow up elsewhere,
But this place isn't all bad,
When you find the one's that care.

There's treasure to be found,
In the mostly unlikely corners,
Oracles and orators,
Crooners and mourners.
More colours than imaginable,
More names than in the scriptures,
In this wonderful little town I'd only heard of on the
football fixtures.

This Christmas Thing

I don't like Christmas.

I love the traditional side of Christmas, whether it be Christian, Pagan or something else. I love the idea of goodwill, of celebrations, spending time with friends and loved ones and singing songs that give you that Christmassy feeling. But I hate the overindulgence, my body's natural instinct to say, "Fuck it, go on, it's Christmas!"

Where would that kind of shit end?

Eating yourself to actual death and getting told off by your ancestors Above and Beyond for being there before your time when you laugh and say, "Aaaah, it's Christmas, in it? You gotta eat loads at Christmas. You gotta drink loads at Christmas. You gotta spend that much money you're still in debt the following December, it's fucking Christmas, mate!"

Present buying is a hassle I could do without.

Kids, okay, normal kids aren't a problem unless they're entitled little pricks who have a list of expensive shit that you'll never be able to afford and will throw hissy fits if they get anything else. My own kids are generally grateful, Martha especially although her tastes and lists are becoming longer and more expensive, but Mortimer can usually be found with a box of unopened presents still on Boxing Day, he's happy just because he's happy. He doesn't need, or want much and that's beautiful.

I think Christmas would be better for everyone if the present buying thing was removed completely, I know that's not possible, and why the hell should it be? I buy the people I love stuff I think they'd like when I see it, I don't need a special occasion other than those two things: I saw this and I love you, and believe me when I buy those presents and they open them the surprise and excitement is better than Christmas and birthday times for both me and recipient.

Here are some Anti-Christmas poems, some piss takes of seasonal hits and some genuinely serious thoughts on 'the most wonderful time of the year.'

It's The Least Wonderful Time Of The Year

It's the least wonderful time of the year,
With the kids bringing home school yard germs,
Giving everyone worms and you're expected to be
full of good cheer,
It's the least wonderful time of the year,

It's the crap-crappiest season of all,
Wishing seasonal best to cunts you detest,
Who you'd much rather maul,
It's the crap-crappiest season of all,
There'll be facebook for posting,
Fake dinners I'm not roasting,
And I'll be praying for no snow,
There'll be long boring hours,
Watching shite get devoured, I
Should have stopped long, long ago,
It's the least wonderful time, it's not cheap,
There'll be no romantic snog,
Just pornhub in the bog,
When everyone's asleep,
It's the least wonderful time of the year,
There'll be parties for skipping,
Black ice for slipping,
And noro-virus fo' sho',
There'll be leery drunk wankers
With overflowing tankards, of
Beer and gin from the sloe,
It's the least wonderful time of the year,
There'll be much money wasted,

And dead animals basted,
And more flab on your rear,
It's the least wonderful time,
Yes, the least wonderful time,
Oh, the least wonderful time,
Of the year

(Christmas)

The snow's comin down
(Christmas) and the weather's appalling
(Christmas) the buses are stalling
(Christmas) babies are bawling
(Christmas) germs are crawling

The shops in the town
(Christmas) are full to the roof beams
(Christmas) full of frustration and screams
(Christmas) and wallets bursting at the seams

They're singing Deck The Halls
But commercially Christmas is balls
'Cause I remember when I had no limits
And my own company and three litres of spirits

There's homeless people on the streets
(Christmas) and over-indulgence between sheets
(Christmas) is all about giving
(Christmas) and remembering those who are still
living.

They're singing Silent Night
But I hate spending money at Christmas, it's shite,
I would rather give things money can't buy,
I buy you stuff the rest of the year, I'm that kind of
guy

If there was a way
(Christmas) I'd abolish physical gift-giving

(Christmas) and try to encourage the living
(Christmas) to practice forgiving

Fast Christmas

Chaos everywhere
Panic in the air
People in maddening no-brainers
Trampling the weak beneath rushing trainers
Hoarding and stocking and stuffing
Food, drink and gifts like they're nothing
Just for one day

A day where I look through the window outside
And look at my view side to side
For a glimmer of the usual life
For normality to cut through the dead world like a
knife
Outside an apocalypse downscaled
Everything shuttered and hidden
The silent world suffocated and paled
As if motion and sound were forbidden

Prisoners in our own home
Prisoners in our own mind
Prisoners if we are alone
Prisoners if we aren't left behind

Eating for something to do
It's Christmas, you're supposed to!
Glutting yourself til you're sick
Killing yourself just a bit that's the trick
We'll undo the damage New Year
After we've drunk all the beer
And gorged ourselves to excess and extreme

Til our guts burst apart at the seam

Worrying about buying something
For the person who has everything
Fighting anxiety and guilt
If you don't have the money there's blood to be spilt

I don't want you to buy me a present
I just want to be in your presence
I don't want to eat, and drink beer
I just want to hear your words in my ear

Merry Christmas

I wanna DO Christmas

I wanna do Christmas by choice,
I wanna sing Christmas songs at the top of my voice.

I wanna wear seasonal clothes,
That feature a Reindeer, red nose,
The Grinch and Gremlins and snows.
I wanna listen to choirs by candle,
And forget about all kinds of scandal,
And and pull my kids on a sled with a handle.
I wanna see cards with victorian singers,
Bonnet-wrapped, merry-making, joy-bringers,
And watch Albert Finney as Scrooge, it's a zinger.

But I want to shut Christmas away,
If I don't feel like celebrating one day,
If troubles have made my heart go astray.
I wanna miss it out now and then,
When the pressure of expectation strikes again,
And it's more than about good will to all men.

I want Christmas to go fuck itself,
When it's more serious than elf on the shelf,
When it's about stripping the poor and stoking the
wealth.

I want Christmas to be about joy,
Like it was when I was but a boy,
Content with or without a new toy.

My Christmas is about love and care,

Showing all I can that I share,
Not necessarily with gifts but by just being there.

It's beginning to look a lot like FUCK THIS!

It's beginning to look a lot like FUCK THIS!
Everywhere I go
Take a look as I walk through town, in Christmas pus
I shall drown
With cheap tacky shite from September onwards

It's beginning to look a lot like FUCK THIS!
Depression is in store
But the shittiest sight to see is the jollyness that will
be
Outside your own front door
Year long family rifts and pointless fucking gifts
Stuff our fat trap
With calorific seasonal crap
Cuz that's what you do,
Even if you've got the flu,
And you consider putting The Samaritans on speed
dial

It's beginning to look a lot like FUCK THIS!
Conjunctivitis in both eyes,
The weather's warming up, Australia's fucked
And we're all wanting mince bloody pies

It's beginning to look a lot like FUCK THIS!
Everywhere I see,
The pressure of pretending I'm happy,
When I'm feeling nothing but crappy
The only snowflakes that are falling

Are the people who're constantly bawling,
About something they want erased from history

It's beginning to look a lot like FUCK THIS!

One more Christmas poem

One more Christmas poem before the big day
One more chance before Santa takes the rein on his sleigh
One more reason to voice my thoughts of the season,
One more chance to commit Christmas treason
One final thing before I feel the big suffocation
The flannelette blanket that forcibly swaddles the nation
One final gasp of pre-Christmas air in my chest,
One last wish for January the 2nd to arrive clean and dressed

One last wish that this year it will be different
That the ghosts will not visit to remind and to torment
Of times long ago when Christmas was magic
Before memories were made and it became tragic

Of miserable bastards at Christmas,
I'm one of the greats,
I'm worse than Ebenezer Scrooge,
And the character in Gremlins played by Phoebe Cates,
I'm furrier than The Grinch and just as green,
Twice as grumpy,
Thrice as mean,
You'll get nothing from me
Not even coal in a sock
Unless it's for me to use
To smack you in the cock

Merry Christmas I suppose,
I hope your day this year is brighter,
If it's not just attack your Christmas tree with some
petrol and a lighter.

Christmas Tree

A
Life.
Stretching,
Growing, reaching
Upwards towards the
Bright and beautiful sun
Seasons on your limbs; Wind
Between splayed digits, Hot sun
On grateful fronds, Rain on withered, thirsty
Roots, Snow accentuating each and every needle
How
Can
They
Cut
You Down?

Xmas Thanks

It's Christmas time,
There's every need to be afraid,
No I'm not here to sing and serenade.
I'm here, full of cheer and no beer,
At this most wonderful time of year to give wanks
and breast fishes to a certain number of you.
At the start of this year I set myself a task,
To get off my quiche,
Shift off my arse.
I bit the bullet and joined a gym,
Determined to go from fat boy to slim.
But none of this would have happened without you
lot,
The names that follow were part of the plot.

First of all Amy for ever resisting,
Endless gifs of chicken fisting.
For inspiring me to join the gym,
That I've never seen her in,
Maybe she should go back,
And get off her quim.

To the boys down the pub who I shall now name,
Offend and abuse unfriend and shame.
Scott Carter for photographing picturesque bike rides
around buildings of various debilitation,
And showing equal enthusiasm for alcoholic
inebriation.

To Richard Archer for reading my shit and stealing
the show,
And rocking all denim like status quo.

To Paul Morris the tall, handsome get,
For being a good friend and not dying yet.

Jonathan Butcher's praise and adoration,
When taking a break from his chronic masturbation.

To little Matt Humphries the cheeky little scamp,
For being a buddy and being a champ,
Organising these events,
Getting frisky in the gents,
Offering me 'his special' for fifty pence.
To his lovely Jo Jo for keeping him grounded,
When secretly I bet he loves his arse pounded.

To the man to whom I wish signed my adoption,
A pint-sized poet with a biblical voice,
A powerful concoction.
My first published author other than myself,
Go buy his book and place it high on your shelf,
Cacophony of Stardust is a name you can trust,
By the legendary Al Barz, a hero, a must!

To the queen of Darlo Leanne Cooper,
For being a friend,
And being a trooper,
For kicking arse,
And being brave,
Helping me drive away the frownies,

When spending time in Darlaston whilst Martha's at
brownies.

James Josiah my running messiah,
For turning my thighs into pistons of fire,
For cheering me on and fueling the pyre,
Consistently quicker making my times higher,
I'd gift you my running shoes soaked through from
endless perspire,
For you to breath in the aroma of the success you
inspire.

To Ian Davies for not being the weirdo I remembered
all them years back.
To Ian Davies for being a weirdo.

To Emma Dehaney my partner in grime,
For making Burdizzo Books the best Burdizzo Books
in all time.
She is a hit shot editor and a true friend and sister,
I walk five hundred miles for her,
Or until I got a blister.

To all the chickens I've eaten since May,
I hope to fuck your ghosts don't come back to haunt
me one day.

To all the hot ladies who work out at the gym,
Sorry for staring it is not what you think,
I get dry eyes when in need for a drink,
And though my mouth is slobbering it's hardly
hydrated,

And I swear that tented area in my shorts is what the
air cons inflated.

To my everloving family, Manjo and the kids,
For putting up with my bumpy journey,
And emotional skids.
Manjo who does more than she does think,
My beautiful wife with her angel crown of pink,
She's the glue that keeps us bonded,
I'm the shit that gets us stuck,
But she's also Elsa with a snowdrift,
And I'm the hero with a truck.
Our demonic little angel,
A devil would not possess,
He'd take one look in a leaf from her book,
And back off cuz the mess.
Martha-Mai is my devil disguised with charm,
An anagram of Martha-Mai is 'I am at harm',
We discovered this after,
Her name it was bestowed,
We worried that we had cursed the girl,
That a jinx on her we had fit,
But we soon learned as she grew up,
It was us who was in the shit,
Painfully intelligent, manipulation extraordinaire,
From the moment she could independently run
amok just in her underwear,
The perfected seething anger and penetrating stare,
And then showing that she loves me, Showing she
does care.
How does she show this?
By kisses, hugs, gifts and art?

No, by pressing her bum on my face and letting rip a
fart.
My little girl is a boy in disguise obsessed with
rudest innuendos,
Pushing her naked buttocks to make shapes in
condensation on the windows.
Cackling like a wicked witch,
Martha-Mai my evil little daughter,
Naughty, cheeky, little git,
I know because I taught 'er!

Mortimer who some of you all of by name,
Though many have not met,
And I guess that's a shame,
I don't hide him away,
He's my happy soul,
My missing jigsaw piece,
Making me whole,
With his routines and rituals,
Not satanic like Martha-Mai,
Just lift, or bus watching, or watching videos all day,
You've come on leaps and bounds,
This year with your new school,
Given yourself and us freedom,
That we all need to refuel,
And for that I thank you,
May school time pass swift,
A fuck all them cunts who moan,
When you mess with the lift!

To all of the people I expected to pressure me to
drink,
What was I thinking?

What did I think?
You're all real friends,
You've helped me along,
You've kept me going,
Made me strong,
Kept me together,
Kept me in line,
Taken the piss,
But hey that's just fine.
To all of the people above and beyond,
I like/love/need/want, delete where appropriate,
you.
You rock my world and I hope I yours too.

The Junkie Before Christmas

Twas the night before Christmas, when all through
the city
Stirred genuine needy, and the vultures of pity;
Money was spent, frivolously without care,
In hopes they would be the most generous there;
The children were nestled, all snug in their beds;
While visions of overpriced presents danced in their
heads;
And Mum's going crazy, wrapping presents
umpteen,
Praying the children won't fall ill and shit out their
spleen.

When out on the landing there arose such a clatter,
I sprang from my bed to see what was the matter.
Away to the spyhole I flew like a flash,
Tore open the shutter and got a strong whiff of hash.
The moon shining in through the frosted, double-
glazed glass
Gave the lustre of midday to the junkie upstairs, on
the floor on his arse,
Not a vision of Santa with his jolly red face,
But a fifty-five year old piss-head who sat in disgrace

With a little cold shiver, so lively and quick,
He took out a syringe and took out his dick.
Then all of a sudden Santa appeared,
All jolly red-faced, round belly and beard
And he crouched down and coaxed, and called the
junkie by name:

"Now, Spencer, my friend aren't you glad that I
came?
Now take a hold of my hand, and you'll feel no more
pain
Come Chancer, come Idiot,
On, Junkie! On User
No more will you be the foul self-abuser!
To the top of the flats! To the roof of this block!
Now dash away! Dash away! Dash away, Chop,
chop, chop."
And Spencer gazed up in a sobering glow
As from the ceiling above glittered magical snow
He raced up the last flight of stairs unawares,
That he'd left his earthly body behind with its
unearthly scares
Up to the rooftop he raced childish glee in his chest
A rustle of sleigh bells increased his zest
A sleigh piled high not with gifts but with love, hope
and dreams,
An endless amount for those who believe
And then, in a twinkling, I heard on the roof
The prancing and pawing of sixteen reindeer hoof.
I looked through the fire exit, no care for myself,
To see Santa dress Spencer the junkie as his chief elf.
He was dressed in green, from his head to his toes,
And his boots were all varnished and sparkled like
his nose.
A look of serenity, of peace, of belonging,
No more hurt, no more wronging

His eyes — how they twinkled! His dimples, how
merry!
His cheeks were like roses, his nose like a cherry!

His droll little mouth was drawn up like a bow,
And the skin on his chin was as clean as a whistle
And his countenance and stance were as sharp as a
thistle
Santa nodded and pointed through clouds at the
moon;
"I'm sorry Spence, boy, for taking you so soon."
Spencer he laughed and grinned ear to ear, "Why
Santa, there's nothing at all left for me here"
Santa clapped Spence on the back and they boarded
the sleigh
Within moments they would be up, up and away
But one last thing was said, as if he knew I were
secretly hearing
And he shouted this before the reindeer flew into the
sky's clearing
"To everyone living whether they're doing it right,
Try not to judge, try not to fight,
For each of us endures life in a unique way to
ourself,
And each one of you has the potential of becoming
an elf"

Anti-Christmas song

Death-nuts roasting on a funeral pyre
Frostbite nipping at your toes
OAPS being mugged by a choir
And homeless dressed up like Eskimos
Everybody knows eating turkey and mistletoe,
Will help to make you see some shite,
Tiny tots with their beds all aglow
Will find it hard to sleep tonight
They know that Satan's on his way
He's loaded lots of tools and demons on his sleigh
And every evil mother's child is gonna learn
What reindeer smells like when it does burn
A sacrificial offering will get you through this simple
phase
Just naughty kids from 1 to 92
Although blood's been shed many times, many ways
Merry Christmas to you
And every mother's child is gonna learn
What reindeer smells like when it does burn
A sacrificial offering will get you through this simple
phase
Just naughty kids from 1 to 92
Although blood's been shed many times, many ways
Merry Christmas, fuck you

OTHER TITLES BY

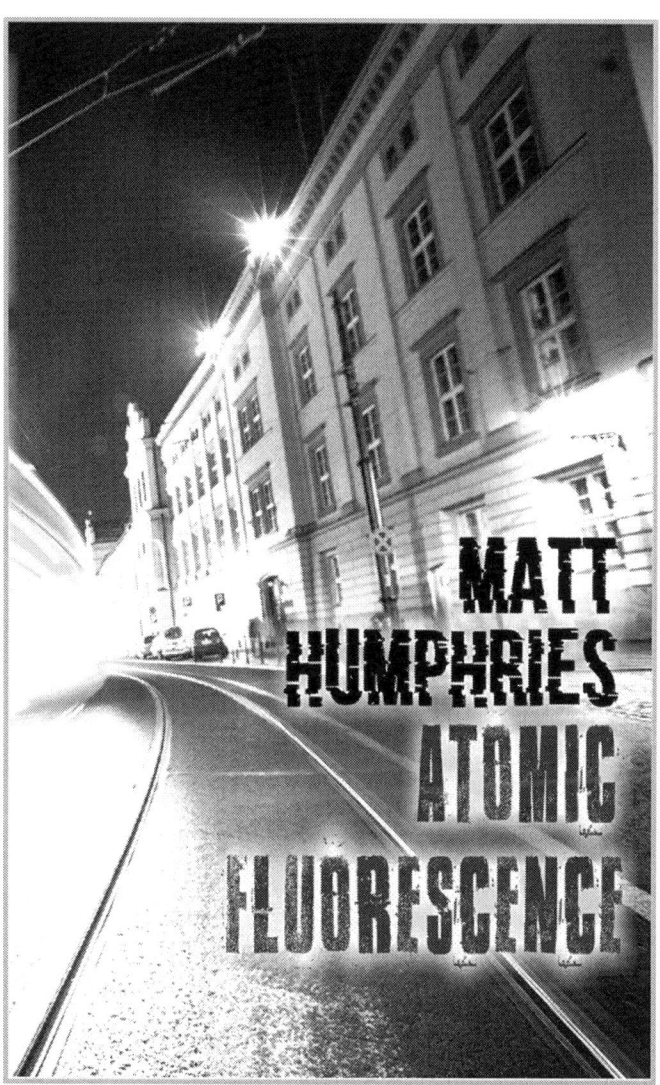

MATT HUMPHRIES ATOMIC FLUORESCENCE

Printed in Great Britain
by Amazon

34931436R00080